Don't Throw Away The Daisies

A collection of poetry
by
Ann Perrin

Ann Perrin

ISBN 978-1-4461-7941-3

Copyright © Ann Perrin, 2010

First Edition

The author asserts the moral right under the Copyright, Designs and Patents Act 1988 to be identified as the author and illustrator of this work.
All Rights reserved. No part of this publication may be reproduced, stored in a retrieval system, or transmitted, in any form or by any means without the prior written consent of the author, nor be otherwise circulated in any form of binding or cover other than that in which it is published and without a similar condition being imposed on the subsequent purchaser.

Don't Throw Away The Daisies

This collection is in memory of my mother

Joan Field.

With love to my long suffering partner Alan Gage, to Robin and Paul Perrin, Sheila, Caroline and John Herbert, my wonderful uncle in California!

Ann Perrin

Index

Impressions   7
Fall of West Pier   9
Auntie Joyce   10
Tender Lunacy   11
The Salt Sea Winds   13
Snow   14
Day Trippers   15
My Garden   17
Midges Dance   18

The House In Highgate   19
The Winning Smile   20
The Legacy   21
Weaving Spells   22
A Widow's Weeds   23
The House in Highgate   24
Granny's Corset   25
Treble Clef   26
The Blue Necklace   27

Transitions   29
Don't Throw Away The Daisies   30
Reconciliation   31
The Oleander   32
Blackpool Sands   33
The Passing Season   34
The Black Bin Bag   35

What A Performance!   37
Beach Combing   38
On The Fiddle   39
I Wish   40
The Marionettes   41

Grandchildren   43
Smiley House   45
The Hole in the Wall   47
The Lost Cat   49

It Matters — 51
Yesterday's News — 52
The Weeping Willow — 53
The Supply Teacher — 54
Fear of Aging — 56
Haikus in Hospital — 57
A and E — 58

Memory — 59
Eating Apricots in France — 60
The Table — 61
Picasso's Model — 62
One Sunday — 63
The Ring — 64

Journeys — 65
Moving On — 66
The Tramp on the Train — 67
Blackpool Illuminations — 69
The Nightmare — 70
Arriving In India — 71
For Monica — 72

Funny Bits — 73
The Green Tights — 74
Once Upon A Time — 76
Ego — 77
The Bus Pass — 78
In Praise of Croydon — 79
A Panic Attack — 80

About the Author — 83

Don't Throw Away The Daisies

Impressions

Ann Perrin

The Fall of the West Pier

Rumbling crushing crumbling
oblivious to reason it moves over pebbles
seeking its prey.
A huge head hovers, steely eye glints
as massive neck swings high in the air
peering over pickings.
Pillars and poles, wrought iron railings
a mountain of memories
in heaps on the beach.

Rumbling crashing crumbling
remnants of the ballroom
like a doomed Titanic fall.

Two giant orange-crab like cranes
crawl from foreshore to the sea
shifting and sifting
through the shingle.
their greedy mouths picking
over the debris where
ribbons of mussels cling.

Flimsy metal window frames
float like disembodied birds
beaten into submission
tossed into lorries for landfill.

A huge tower of steel and glass
will be its tombstone.
Long queues will make their way
for a chance to glance
at an uncertain landscape.

Rumbling crashing crumbling.

"Doesn't it look tidy now?"
says a passer-by.

Ann Perrin

Auntie Joyce

A liking for stew swimming
with mutton and barley.
Or was it because it went a long way
with a family to feed
in those post-war years?

Adored wife of a faithful husband,
whose gentle humour held a
happy family together, who worked
most of his life for Kelloggs.

A respectable, responsible couple,
pillars of the community,
firm and forthright on the outside,
soft and smiley on the inside,
laughter her legacy.

Tender Lunacy

Lying in tangled confusion
willing the phone to ring

The wind in the tree outside
is more purposeful than I

The book so wilfully abandoned
tells of a life more meaningful

Self inflicted misery
plays its music repeatedly

What tender lunacy leaves
its victim waiting so patiently?

Ann Perrin

The Salt Sea Winds

Where salt sea winds make their eerie sounds
and grey-green waves come crashing to the shore
and water washed pebbles tumble from obscurity
into an ever changing collage of muted colour.

High on the shore, a beached starfish lies rigid in the sun,
greedy seagulls eat oysters, leaving empty shells abandoned,
bobbly brown seaweed mingles with ribbons of green,
chalky cuttlefish lie beside a shiny skate egg husk.

One pebble, grey and white - with a gleam of light
shining through its centre, a shape, strangely soothing.

Rolled over in the palm of my hand its hard cold surface
seems like a symbol of something mystic, other worldly.

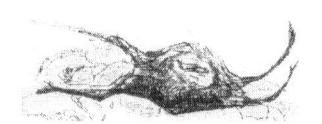

Ann Perrin

Snow

A fine white veil falls
over the face of the world
slowly freezing time.

Day Trippers

Here they come streaming out of the station
and down to the sea
where squawky seagulls herald their arrival.

Ignoring stripy deckchairs at wind breaks
they settle for their beach mats and
home-grown towels.

Barefoot children brave the pebbles
to meet the chill of the sea,
throw stones to skim the waves.

Kites flutter with over optimistic gaze
ice creams melt,
tea in paper cups turns cold.

Too soon the fun comes to an end
and nervous crabs in buckets
await their fate.

But all is well,
everything is packed
children sent to discharge their captives.

Ann Perrin

My Garden

I could sit here in my garden
all my waking hours,
simply entranced
by the profusion
of flowers.

Clouds of blue wisteria
float above my head,
and Aquilegia pink and mauve
frame where the birds are fed.

Pansies almost tumble
from my unruly pots,
and spring bulbs left to sleep awhile,
obscure forget-me-nots.

The cherry blossoms sprouting
before the bluebells fade away
and roses gather all their strength
to make a good display.

The passion flower is teasing
the ivy round the tree,
lily of the valley
share their scent with me.

I could sit here in my garden
all my waking hours,
simply entranced
by the profusion
of flowers.

Midges dance

Dragonflies with translucent wings hover,
Green grubs wriggle under water lily leaves,
A white butterfly struggles for freedom in a spider's web,
Bees fill their socks with pollen from summer flowers,
Midges dance in the failing evening light.

The House in Highgate

Ann Perrin

The Winning Smile

On a warm sunny Sunday I slipped from my mother's womb,
greeted by the buzz of bombs.
London in the middle of a war, a baby with blue eyes
and a cleft palate.
But my smile soothed the souls of burned and bandaged soldiers,
talking only with their eyes.

My mother sought lodgings in Wales
near father's barracks, alien territory, to say goodbye
before his active service.
In forlorn kitchens on grimy stoves she heated milk.
I coughed and choked as she poured warm waves of milk
from a tiny spoon.

Poor mother, a girl caught on tenuous threads of life.
Later, curled up together, our mutual dependency
slumbered in the silence of the night.

The Legacy

Crawling through debris of their lives,
no trenches,
just the aftermath of war.

No mention of stoic grandfathers,
of gas filled lungs
or broken spirits.

Our parents inheritance,
optimism and endeavour,
a new world emerges.

But not for long.
Soon fathers and sons
will fight again on foreign shores.

Rootless marriages collapse
despite the power and passion,
children retreat, sober and thoughtful.

May we yet turn the corner
and discover sufficient fertile soil
to flower and grow?

Unexpected blooms thrive in dry stone walls
and carpets of colour transform
the battlegrounds of the past.

Ann Perrin

Weaving Spells

He was a magician to us
weaving spells with wood and clay.
Other people's dads went to work
and reappeared for supper.

Ours spent his days
and most nights
carving marionettes
in his cluttered workshop.

He was always engrossed
kneading clay or carving wood,
the music of Glen Miller blaring
from a battered radio.

We would clink through the chaos
with mother's homemade cakes,
the smell mingling with the stench of glue
boiling on an ancient cooker.

Our faces shone with shy smiles
as his hand took the teacup.
He had been whisked away to war,
we barely knew him.

We lived at Gran's
and discovered him one day
in the hallway
with a battered trunk.

A soldier
in a coarse khaki uniform,
a clarinet in a case
and chocolate in his pockets.

A Widow's Weeds

Mrs Howell had always lived in the attic
in her widow's weeds.
We children swore she wore them in bed
and wondered how she managed up there
without a lavatory.
Once a month the coalman called
with his horse and cart
tumbled coal from a sooty bag
into the tiny cupboard on her landing
One day I sat on her stairs,
listening to her fire fizz
as she jabbed it with a poker.
Shocked when she opened the door
and said softly "Would you like to come in?"

A tiny room with a high bed,
a chest of drawers, a primus stove,
a washstand, a shelf of little treasures.
I looked up at the sloping window
in the roof, all she had were clouds
to keep her company.
She showed me her pieces of seaside
pottery, a photo of a man in a uniform,
a cut-glass dish pasted with a picture
of Niagara Falls.

I held the dish up to the skylight.
Kaleidoscope colours danced around the room.
I saw the warmth of her smile,
heard the ripple of her laughter.
But time had vanished, I had to go.
Mrs Howell was wrapping a newspaper parcel
wrapping and rolling.
Rolling paper round and round
I was doubtful but she insisted.

Sixty years ago
And I still have the glass dish
The Falls are long gone but the
kaleidoscope of colours remain
and ripples of her laughter
still dance in my mind.

Ann Perrin

The House in Highgate

Peter Pan had a lot to answer for!
We were always sliding down the polished
banisters and leaping off at the last minute
in our everlasting efforts to fly.

We spent half our lives on the stairs,
creating stories about the paintings
that hung from floor to ceiling in the hall.

Listening to the chip-chip-chipping of
the wood in father's workshop
as he made his marionettes
and the whizz and whirr of mother's Singer
sewing seams for debutants dresses.

Real boredom had us mimicking
arguments outside auntie and uncle's door.
Mother would have had a fit if she had known
as we rushed and locked ourselves in the lavatory.

Auntie advanced demanding apologies.
Too late, we were balancing on the pan
and then leaping out of the tiny window
into the security of the garden.

How I loved that house.

Granny's Corset

Push open the door and enter her room
with heavy beige wallpaper
and brown gloss paint.

Grandma, propped up with pillows,
crisp white sheet,
pure silk eiderdown,
raises a frail hand in greeting.

Time to cram her into her corset,
I stagger from chair to bed
with the well washed cotton contraption.
I am eight and grown up.
I fasten the buckles, thread tapes,
tug at cords, clip on suspenders,
under her orderly instructions.

I help her into her flowery frock,
brush her hair, dab on some powder,
pass her a mirror for her approval.
A bomb damaged Grandma's back
but mother says she is indomitable.
She glides downstairs ready
to organise the rest of the house.

Ann Perrin

It flows so easily from my hand,
this treble clef of yours, copied
so many times, as if making it
would bring back the sound of
you playing your precious piano.

Eyes shut, you would escape to your
younger days when the world seemed
so full of opportunity, just for
a few notes in the right places.

Swinging with the beat of your
beloved jazz or, as swiftly, changing
tune to a romantic melody.

Returning to the room where
our discordant singing rang
through your reverie, knowing,
as you always had, that
the present is but a shadow of those
innocent days of your youth.

The Blue Necklace

Abandoned in the bottom of a box
beads of azure blue,
my eyes close,
willing the memory to return.

Yes, I can see her now -
those teasing eyes,
her dark brown hair,
satin gown and silver shoes.

And for tonight,
just for tonight,
grandmother's treasured necklace
gracing her slender throat.

A smile, a kiss and she is gone,
gone to dance with father,
to an unfamiliar peacetime tune,
her perfume drifting into the night.

Ann Perrin

Don't Throw Away The Daisies

Transitions

Ann Perrin

Don't Throw Away The Daisies
for Gwen

Thank you for passing the time with me,
It's so lonely waiting to die.

Can't tell you how angry I felt
when you first appeared
with fruit and flowers
wittering on about sun and the seasons?

I wanted to scream at you *'I'm dying.'*
Have you got the colouring book?
One of your slightly better ideas.
Silly really but I love doing them,
reminds me of being little,
using every crayon in the box.
Mother and me at the kitchen table.

Now when you do the flowers,
please don't throw away the daisies,
although I know they are past their best.

Could you do my nails?
I often had a manicure when I was working,
it seems important that God should see
I've tried my hardest.

I love the oils, the scent of lavender
challenging that mournful medical smell.

Hold my hand, I'm feeling so very tired.

Deep rhythms overwhelm me
creeping in on every side.

My eyelids are amazing rainbows,
how very strange.

Let's say goodbye now – softly -
just in case I slip away.

Reconciliation

Seeds take flight with the softest blow,
on dandelion clocks you know.

Forever?

How long can that be?
And who's in charge of time. Tell me?

Twin spirits drift and sometimes fly,
but cannot separate or die.

Distance is all in the mind,
a word for space I think you'll find.

Alienation is a choice,
but takes an angry tone of voice.

Despite the walls, the gates, the locks,
think of the seeds around that clock.

They drift, they fly, they find some ground,
and safely grow until they're found.

Ann Perrin

The Oleander

We found it in Albi,
no gentle sketch
but boldly painted
bright and blowzy
heady with scent,
out for a good time.

In London.
loving the culture
pink petals
flirted with passers-by
revelled in attention
posed for pictures.

Uprooted to Brighton
in a white fleece shroud
it faltered
leaves fell
naked boughs mourned
sensing life had passed.

Two years later
in a new pot
on a south facing wall
tiny green shoots emerge,
pink blossoms
show their party faces.

Don't Throw Away The Daisies

Blackpool Sands

The beach is a seascape of magic
the wind sings a song in the air.
Sand seems to go on forever,
in the distance the pier and the fair.

The thud of the hooves as we canter,
our hearts beating faster at speed,
faces flushed with exertion,
as my sister takes up the lead.

We slow down and splash along shoreline,
hands on the reins check the pace.
When the journey of life takes us forward,
we'll remember this time and this place.

Ann Perrin

The Passing Season

Hidden from view he hums,
deep resonant sounds of age and wisdom.
My neighbour's steady beat on wooden stakes
marks time to his labour and his tune.

I peer into my wintered pond for life,
heavily pregnant newts glide in waiting.
Bluebells challenge crocuses for their space,
buds of blossom spring from spiky branches.

Ash tree seeds scatter in the wind,
making space for waving fronds of green.
Birds compete for feathers for their nests.
The capricious sun hides its features.

A silence falls on secret thoughts,
as winter's drama melts away at last.

The Black Bin Bag

Darker than she remembered
with a beige patterned rug,
threadbare in places.

Porcelain figurines with frozen smiles
gaze out at her from their
well polished walnut cabinet.

The cutlery nestled in the drawer of the dresser
reminds her of the happy family
meals they had shared.

She pulls back the floral curtains
watches the sun's rays
dancing on the white walls.

A wedding photo in a silver frame
family faces smile down at her,
making her task seem more bearable.

On a whim
she spills the contents of a drawer
on the floor and sits down to sort them.

A Christmas angel, a little brass bell,
a buckle, an old bunch of keys
a brooch with a broken clasp.

She fingers each one slowly
knowing in her heart
its history has been abandoned.

She moves into the kitchen
where the smell of herbs
still linger.

Recipes carefully cut from magazines,
a jar of string, a decorated cake tin
slippers on the floor next to the back door.

It all has to go, she shakes
the residue of a life
into a black bin bag.

Ann Perrin

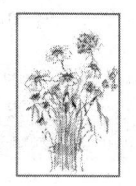

Don't Throw Away The Daisies

What A Performance!

Ann Perrin

Beachcombing

Where a solitary seagull flew,
hopeful of an unexpected catch,
an old man moved along
the deserted seashore,
glancing skywards,
as if to ward off new invaders.

He kept his gaze low,
pausing then pouncing,
hands sifting piles of slippery pebbles,
"Makes a good walk" he called,
digging to retrieve his bounty -
two battered 20p coins.

"Like poetry?"
he called, I nodded,
so with one hand cupped
to the side of his mouth,
warding off competition
from the roar of the wind
on the incoming tide,
he launched into a sonnet.

His words swooped, soared,
glided past present reality
and far out to sea,
I clapped respectfully
as he continued to work the beach
as a showman might,
reaping his due rewards for such
a powerful performance.

On The Fiddle

Playing the fiddle
he walks the tightrope
strung between two lamp posts.

With over painted mouth
and yellow hair
dancing attendance
his bow catches
an uncertain sound
drowned by the man
with the band
playing the blue tuba
outside the Pavilion.

He tempts and teases
smiles down at passers-by

Later he waits for the bus
catches his reflection
in a window
a painted smile and
black crossed eyes
stare back.

In his tiny attic room
the show is over
his image melts in the mirror
with Crows Cremine
and Kleenex tissues.

Time for a beer and to disappear!

Ann Perrin

I Wish

My dad works in the circus
And when we go to school
He shows me lots of circus tricks,
He likes to play the fool.

Miss Chivers showed him round one day,
He cartwheeled in the gym
And swung on ropes above our heads
So we all laughed at him.

Mr Potts was cleaning windows
When dad was going round,
He put a bucket on his head
Two metres from the ground.

He juggled in the classroom
With books and balls and rings
And balanced boxes on his nose
And other clever things.

Mrs Pie was in the kitchen
Dad loves to help with flour.
He made some lovely custard pies.
Which passed a pleasant hour.

Miss Chivers said "It's time to go"
But dad was having fun
So he strung us up a tightrope,
We practised one by one.

But now we have to do our work
So dad will have to go,
Will he listen? Not my dad,
He's swinging to and fro.

The Marionettes

When the velvet curtain rises,
music sets the scene,
characters from wonderland
unfold their curious theme.

Promised paths and gardens,
a walk with talking flowers,
a busy running rabbit,
a mushroom's magic powers.

A strange Mad Hatter, in a rant
makes all the tea things shake,
a dormouse in a teapot
cannot stay awake.

A droopy jawed old Duchess,
a Queen who loves to shout,
knaves who paint the roses
when no-one is about.

The puppets strut about the stage,
then hang back in their rows,
a never ending circle
of summer season shows.

Ann Perrin

Grandchildren
for Joshua, Jamie and Nicky

Ann Perrin

Smiley House
Joshua

We are off to Granny's beach hut
so we are waiting for the train,
with buckets, balls and sandwiches,
umbrellas for the rain.

Gran says we'll walk for ages,
so the buggy's just in case.
My legs are not quite long enough
to walk at Granny's pace.

Gran talks and talks to all her friends,
so I wait patiently,
But now we empty everything
because she's lost the key.

At last we open Smiley House,
The name is on the door,
It's full of lots of lovely things
and I've been here before.

There are nets to do the fishing,
a kettle for Gran's tea,
a chair for her to take a rest while I
throw pebbles in the sea.

If I want a paddle
I have to tell my Gran,
I'm not allowed to go alone,
She has to hold my hand.

We eat up all the sandwiches,
At four we catch the train,
We've had a really lovely time
and now here comes the rain!

Ann Perrin

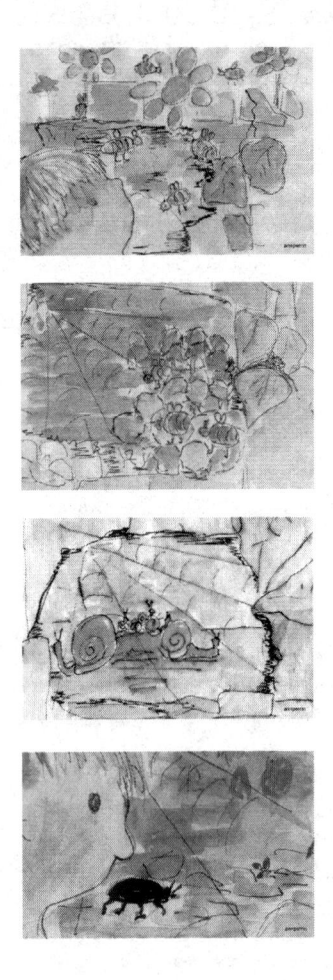

The Hole in the Wall
Jamie

There is a garden I know,
with an old dry stone wall.

I wonder who lives there,
perhaps no one at all.

Maybe a spider with spots brown and gold,
a mouse with a family to keep from the cold.

A slithery snake could climb into the gap,
a hedgehog curl up for a long winter nap.

The hole is quite dark so I can't really see
but I think there are eyes staring right back at me.

It could be a toad and this is his home
or a safe place for snails until babies have grown.

For bees it is handy because they like flowers,
they could make lots of honey which takes hours and hours.

But why not a dragon who blows fire and smoke
or a home for a gnome and magical folk?

A shifty black beetle runs past my nose,
if I watch him quite carefully I'll will see where he goes.

The floor is all earthy but I think I can see,
spotty brown toadstools as far as can be.

In the roof there's a crack with a wee bit of light
where a ladybird likes to crawl up and take flight.

Butterflies might want to hide from the rain,
rest for a while and fly off again.

There is a garden I know with an old dry stone wall,
I wonder who lives there, perhaps no one at all.

Ann Perrin

The Lost Cat
Nicky

The cat on our wall
is shaggy and brown.
I've been trying to reach him
but he won't come down.

He looks soft and furry,
his eyes sharp and bright
as he watches the birds
from morning to night.

He's washing his fur
while I'm eating my tea,
I pretend that he's mine
and his name's Gregory.

Mum says she is sorry,
but he can't come indoors
he is somebody else's
and has muddy paws.

He meowed at my window
and made such a din,
I opened it up
and let him climb in.

Mum made him a label
and put up a sign,
if nobody claims him
perhaps he'll be mine.

Mum says "Don't be hopeful,
he's somebody's cat,
and when they collect him
that will be that."

Ann Perrin

It Matters

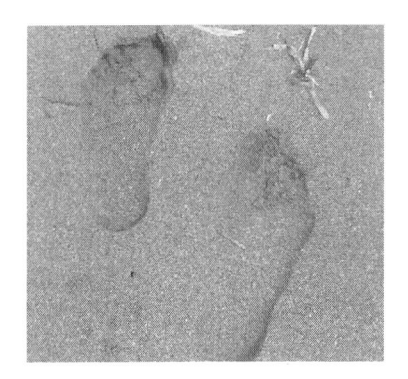

Ann Perrin

Yesterday's News

Picking their way through bricks and debris
burnt relics of family life
seeking just a small memento,
a photo of a loved one's face
gazes up through shards of glass
frozen in time
the last symbol
of safety,
shattered.

The Weeping Willow

The weeping willow
weeps no more
an ugly stump marks its passing
kindred spirits
sing songs
in the wind

Ann Perrin

The Supply Teacher

The tall inspector entered
on her half day as supply,
Charlie threw a tantrum
and she couldn't find out why.

She tried to keep some order
as the lesson had begun,
she'd set them all some writing
and the story sounded fun!

It was about a special sandwich
for sufferers of greed,
with lots of creepy crawlies,
so spelling they would need.

"Settle down now, quickly"
she said, and read the book,
glaring hard at Charlie
who had a treacherous look.

When they'd finished writing
they'd make some paper springs,
for a different kind of sandwich
with lots of cut-out things.

The brushes were all slimy
as they sloshed them in the glue,
the tables were a sticky mess.
and all the children too.

Tom hid in the cupboard
while they sorted out the mess,
he refused to come out ever
although she tried her best.

Some water in the corner
made a merry sound
as Charlie washed up all the pots,
it splashed onto the ground.

Then suddenly they settled
and as if to make amends,
all the work got finished
and everyone was friends.

Don't Throw Away The Daisies

With sodden shoes, the inspector
headed for the door,
saying "Must try harder,
there are only thirty-four."

Tom helped to clean the classroom,
and she was fair but firm,
but her teacher's heart had left her,
never to return.

So to all you tall inspectors
we hope your shoes are dry,
for we work daily miracles
and you're just passing by.

Ann Perrin

Fear of Aging
Pricked and pumped
rolled and kneaded
shoved and shifted
dropped and dangled
watered and barely fed.
Dying without dignity.

Haikus in hospital

She'd lived in France near the Somme
vast experience
there for the talking.

Tortured burbling
comforted into silence,
they say she's pretty

Ann Perrin

A and E

Walking, talking, Friday, jaunting,
pubbing, clubbing, take the train,
mixing, meeting, shagging, gagging,
drinking, sinking, what a shame.
Bottles flying,
someone's crying,
cut and bleeding,
what a fight,
swopping stories,
sharing glories –
A and E
on Friday night.

Don't Throw Away The Daisies

Memory

Ann Perrin

Eating Apricots in France
for Jean and Mado

Under the sun umbrella
on the terrace
old friends meet.

Watching the mist on mountains
listening to the call of the cowman
urging his herd to milking.

Eating apricots, sipping wine,
a gentle informality,
born of shared memories.

Don't Throw Away The Daisies

The Table
For Charles and Michelle

When I sit at your table
it's a joy to behold
the wood is well seasoned
so dark and so old.

I can't help consider
the life of the tree
that finished its life
for this table we see.

The man with a saw
who worked in the heat,
the craftsmen whose tools
produced such a feat.

The person with vigour
that polished the grain,
the home for the table,
to which it then came.

The food on the table
and by whom it was made,
the children who helped
and by whom it was laid

So if quarrels arise
or times hard or sad,
remember this table
and the memories we've had.

So the life of the tree
did not end in vain
because family and friends
will share meals again.

Ann Perrin

Picasso's Model

He watches me intently
as though drawing a vase.
I heat my iron once again,
cover the handle with cloth
and continue my labour.

He can't paint the music
of my iron
as it hisses with the heat
or the movement
of my body
as I dance in my mind.

Once I shared his bed
and curled between these sheets
feeling his hands on my smooth
white breasts,
his body firm against mine
as we shared our love
into the night.

Who lies in his studio now
or shares his bed?
I don't ask.
I am just a poor woman
and have nowhere else to go.

One Sunday

The smile is the same smile
his eyes a warm greeting.
We all stand together
"Be seated."
We pray.

Our sons with their children
are all that unite us.
Our love's a past life.
The hymn fades away.

And who are these young men
standing beside him?
Sons from his new life?
"Be seated."
We pray.

Reflections about us
may mirror the changes.
Is my face less fair
than it was in our day?

But time for more singing.
We all stand together,
united in action.
There's nothing to say.

Our grandson is christened
the godparents worthy,
the cameras are clicking
to capture this day.

Is his smile the same smile
or are his eyes misty?
On this special Sunday,
our last chance to pray.

Ann Perrin

The Ring

She said that I should have it
long before she died
and slipped it off her finger,
'It will not fit', I lied.

Facets of the diamond shone
like sun upon the sea.
She knew I'd always loved that ring
and was giving it to me.

She took my hand in her hand
I caught her gentle smile.
We looked at it together
silent for a while.

I could not share my worry
I didn't want to say
that if I took her diamond ring
I might steal her soul away.

Journeys

Ann Perrin

Moving On

Luggage abandoned in the hall
and trains won't wait for late departure.

But here we sit
lost in the dance of life.

Mirrored in this tiny drama
and willing it never to end.

The heat of the fire
lulls us into companionable silence.

The flames leap and flare
reminding us of past passion.

Logs shift and fall
but we are motionless.

Showers of feathery dust
and final embers fall away.

We rise reluctantly to go
and face our fond farewells.

As if in a dream
fading into uncertain futures.

The Tramp On The Train

Watery blue pools of eyes
shone with childlike intensity.
A woollen hat, with knitted brim
ensured a certain dignity.
Trousers secured with knotted tie,
but shoes polished to perfection!
A simple backdrop
to life's little drama.

Bony hands brushed his beard,
recalling the caress
of a past love?

In the train,
he leaned across the seats,
about to lie between them.
Instead, he raised his lager
as a young woman entered.
A silent salute,
born of better days!

Much later in my soft warm bed
I think of him
journeying to and fro
into the night.
Those watery blue eyes denying
me sleep.

Ann Perrin

Don't Throw Away The Daisies

Blackpool Illuminations

How can we sleep, sleep with this din
when all that is out there wants to come in?
The windows ajar so the curtains are free,
ripples of moonlight dance on the sea.

A huge paddle steamer trundles along
with thousands of lights it moves through the throng.
It comes creeping along on the tracks of the tram
cars all start hooting because there's a jam.

Songs from the old days are blaring out loud
every so often they're sung by the crowd.
The brightest of colours, red, blue and green
flick on and off to highlight each scene.

An enormous Mad Hatter is pouring some tea
and pirates trap lost boys under a tree.
Witches and wizards are busy with spells,
goblins and fairies are living in wells.

The boat is upon us and dazzles our eyes,
we find ourselves falling like kites in the skies.
On a giant helter-skelter we find ourselves slide,
we're twisting and turning enjoying the ride.

On candyfloss mountains we'll bounce and we'll jump,
on lollypop twisters we'll land with a thump.
We'll spin round and round on pink and white twirls
and sail the dark seas on liquorice swirls.

We'll stop and have tea that the Mad Hatter makes,
run after the knave who steals all the cakes.
We'll follow the piper who gets rid of the rats,
stroke the soft fur of the fairyland cats.

The boat trundles on to the end of the track,
it's lucky for us that it makes its way back.
So we leave magic dragons and fish that can talk,
three little pigs who are out for a walk.

We pass by our window and take a great leap,
tired with excitement we soon fall asleep.
Our sheets made of cotton have mud here and there,
to remind us at daybreak we really were there.

Ann Perrin

The Nightmare

I can hear a dog howling
as I walk up
an ancient weathered
stone staircase.
Moving steadily
up and up,
round and round,
Up and up.
Don't I know this place?
Yes. It's a bad place to be.
I try to wake up,
It doesn't work,
I am still moving,
round and round,
up the stairs to the
heavy oak door.
Wake up! Wake up!
Stop this now!
Too late!
The door creaks open and
here is the old woman
who looks like a witch,
long white hair and bony fingers.
I know that spinning wheel,
the one that whirls away,
its twisted threads drawing me
towards them.
It's not too late,
WAKE UP!
Please…just open your eyes!
But no,
I am next to the old hag and
my finger is bleeding.
Now I am falling,
falling into oblivion.
The dog stops howling.

Arriving in India

The heat sucked life out of her body
her skin felt strangely numb
heartbeat quickening
lungs full of heavy heat.

Eyes strain
a desperate need to keep focused
as her whole body succumbed to fatigue.

So this is India.
Can death be this simple?

Lost in the mountains, our voices call out
The sky is dark, lit by a million stars.
We cease to care if anyone finds us.

On the Ganges,
boats made of banana leaves,
with tiny tea lights
bounce on the waves.
Taking the souls of loved ones
to a secret destination.

Ann Perrin

For Monica

There were no bells.
Just a woven wicker basket
and Communion.

Hymns, prayers prayed
and a convoy to a muddy field,
where the priest donned his cassock in the rain.

Don't Throw Away The Daisies

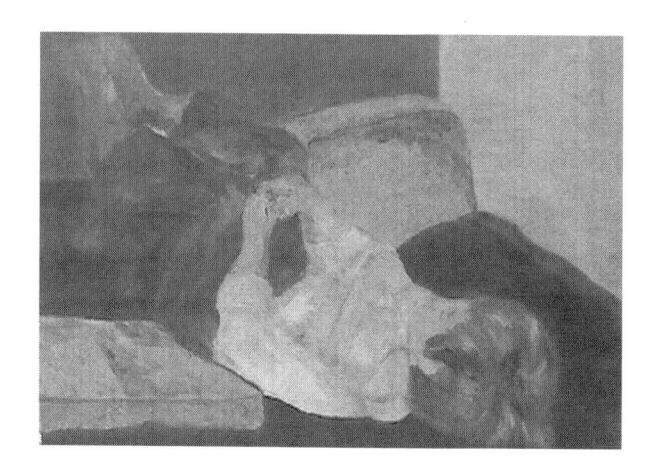

Funny Bits

Ann Perrin

The Green Tights

The king was feeling tetchy;
he did not like the cold.
He had to wear his socks in bed
which made him feel so old.

The Queen said, "Get up darling
you've got to rule the land,"
and swept out to cut some roses
with secateurs in hand.

The Princess Pearl was dreaming
of a Prince down by the lake.
With bug eyed frogs, without a spell,
this was a big mistake.

The jester was in love with her;
he saw his chance at last.
He slipped into some fetching tights,
put on a froggy mask.

From a draughty castle window
the King saw a sorry sight,
a jumping green court jester
with very manly thighs.

The princess said "For goodness sake
I know you are a fake",
and pushed the hapless jester
into the froggy lake.

The King called "Stop this nonsense,
but where did you get those tights?
They look so warm and cosy
they would keep me warm at night."

The Queen called out "I'll knit you some
but you've got a land to rule.
So please my dear get on with it
while I rescue the poor fool.".

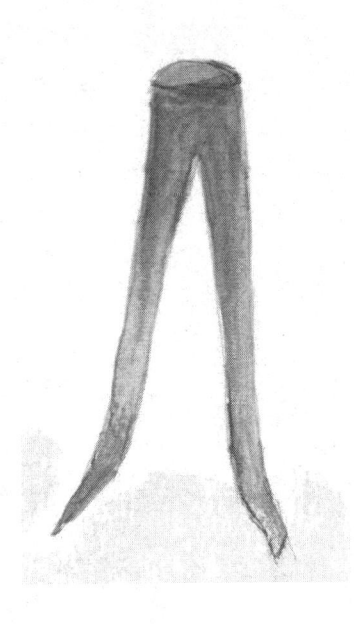

Don't Throw Away The Daisies

The Princess started laughing
at the poor jester's fate,
as a handsome prince came riding
(well he would wouldn't he?)
up to the castle gate.

He was tired of slaying dragons
and the queen had got a net.
So the jester jumped right into it
and everyone got wet.

The Princess and Prince were married
and the king is warm in bed,
wearing long green woolly tights
and his crown upon his head.

The Queen now runs their kingdom
with a dragon's enterprise.
Her right hand man's a jester
which comes as no surprise.

Ann Perrin

Once Upon A Time

Once upon a time
lived a wizened little witch
who loved to interfere with things
she really was a bitch.

Princesses in their castles
who are looking for a bloke,
best beware of evil spells,
the kind that end in croak.

Goblins in their grottos
should always take great care,
she'll steal their hoards
of golden coins, although it isn't fair.

A stupid boy with magic beans
who dreams of wealth and fame,
best not get near witchy poo
she'd surely spoil his game.

And as for ugly sisters
guess who's on their side?
Soppy Cinderella
will never be a bride.

Wolves who eat up children
on her healthy eating ploy,
can collect up special tokens
and trade them for a boy

This witch is very crafty
and may appear a friend.
Be careful what you wish for
and come to a sticky end.

Ego

Ego likes to get about
to jump, to hop, to run,
he's bright and sharp and sparky,
intent on having fun.

When he's at a party
he's rude, he's crass, a bore,
if there is a silence
he'll always take the floor.

Favourite colours red or gold,
he feeds on chocolate cake,
he doesn't like to take a nap,
he needs to stay awake.

He likes to keep abreast of things,
he must be in the know,
he's always in the fast lane,
forever on the go.

Ego's never lonely,
he's busy with his schemes,
he doesn't waste his time on guilt,
he's always full of beans.

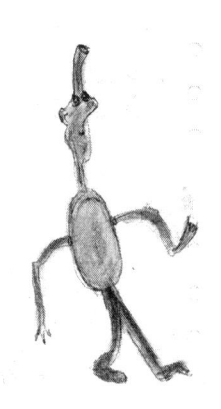

Ann Perrin

The Bus Pass

I've got myself a wheelie bag,
bought granny pants and vests,
accepted that my hair is grey
and started taking rests.

My smile's benign when people call,
but the chain is on the door.
Although they tell you God's about,
I cannot be too sure.

My baby-sitting list is long,
so I won't have the time,
to watch the box or sew and knit
but that will suit me fine.

I'll get my fish on Tuesdays,
it's cheap on pension day,
I won't bother with the housework
because no one comes to stay.

I'll ride along the coastline,
with my free pass for the bus,
drink and smoke and eat my tea
and swear if there's a fuss.

I'll lobby politicians
refuse to go in care.
Would they swop their lot for mine?
I shouldn't think they'd dare.

Getting old is awful,
I'm sinking without trace,
my waist is getting thicker,
deep lines run down my face.

So I'll slap on lots of make up,
wear silk against my skin,
put some highlights in my hair
and find some sex and sin.

In Praise of Croydon

Arty party girls from Highgate,
In the media, on TV.

Tufnel Park is super trendy,
Obviously the place to be.

Feng Shui's spreading over Finchley,
Crystals swing in Camden Town.

Converted warehouse, loft apartments,
Along the river can be found.

In the south we try our hardest,
With Tate Modern and the Wheel.

Dinosaurs still lurk in Dulwich,
But dear old Croydon has appeal.

Parks and gardens, art and drama,
Many ways to spend your time.

Happy shopping, tram stop popping,
To everything you want to find.

Ann Perrin

A Panic Attack

I catch the train in seconds
am breathless when I stop
but did I leave the iron on,
eggs boiling in a pot?
Once a niggling doubt begins
the journey is a blank,
there's water flowing from the bath
emptying the tank.
The bathroom ceiling's
in the lounge
the goldfish flip and flap,
cat's eating them for breakfast
before he takes a nap.
The water's fused the electric,
it's dark as well as wet.
I'm searching for my mobile
it's bad as it can get.
It isn't in my pocket, it isn't in my bag
did I drop it on the bus?
Am I going mad?
Now I see the house ablaze,
the iron has burned the board
but great, I've found my mobile
so thank you, thank you Lord.
Press my neighbour's number,
hurry up please do.
"Now can you check the kitchen
the ironing and the loo?"
Now head in hand I'm praying,
no problems will be found.
Thank God she's back and telling me
things are safe and sound.
I'm sitting smiling on the train
happy with my lot
grateful for small mercies.
Oh damn!
I've missed my stop

Don't Throw Away The Daisies

Ann Perrin

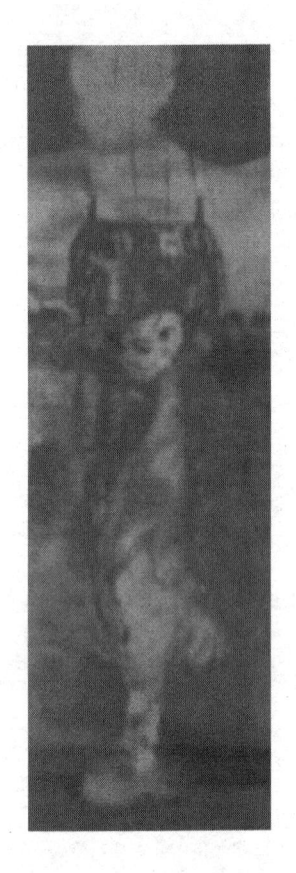

Ann Perrin

Ann comes from a family of marionette makers and performers, and so benefited from living in a creative household.

Ann had a career in the theatre for several years, but when she became a single parent, she decided to qualify as a teacher. She also studied part time to gain a BA and an MSc before moving on to become a lecturer in an Adult Education Institute. Following this she worked as a freelance journalist, as well as having her poems published in various anthologies. She is a member of The Society of Women Writers and Journalists. Her play 'Travelling Nowhere' was performed at the Young Vic.

Around this time, Ann also became an NLP therapist with a practice in London. She has been a carer for two members of her family at different times, which has added to her wide range of life experience.

Currently she paints, writes, makes films and is working on a comedy performance in Brighton, UK.

Acknowledgements

Thanks to John McCullough, Janet Cameron and Jane Maker, for their support and encouragement. Thanks also to Kiersty Boon for her advice and technical expertise in making this publication possible.

Ann Perrin